PIC.

CW01500195

Introduction to a
Neurodiverse World

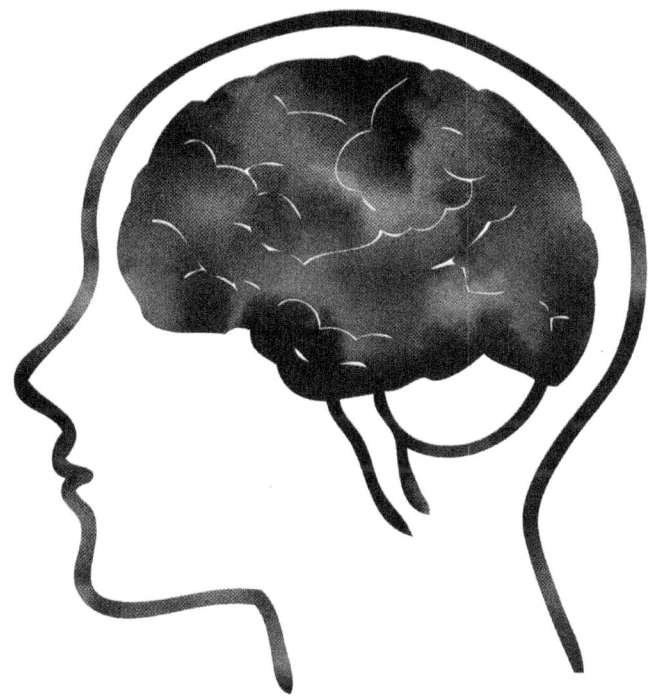

Gareth Croot

Published by Divergent Consultants

Foreword

They say you are what you eat. I must be a mix of plastic, wood and rubber.

Contents

Chapter 1: Introduction to Pica

Pica is a relatively rare eating disorder characterized by the persistent ingestion of non-food substances. These substances can include anything from dirt, clay, and chalk to hair, paper, and ice. While the precise prevalence of pica is difficult to determine due to underreporting and varying definitions across studies, it is estimated that between 4% and 26% of people with intellectual disabilities and up to 24% of pregnant women may experience pica. Despite this, pica is still poorly understood and often stigmatized, with many misconceptions about its causes, consequences, and treatment. This chapter provides an overview of pica, including its historical background, current prevalence in the UK, misconceptions, and definitions.

Historical Background

The term "pica" comes from the Latin word for magpie, a bird that is known for its indiscriminate appetite. The condition has been recognized for thousands of years, with early accounts dating back to ancient Greece and Rome. Pica has been documented in a wide range of cultures and contexts, from African and Asian tribes to Western societies. Some anthropologists have even suggested that pica may have played a role in human evolution, as it may have helped early humans to adapt to nutrient-poor environments by providing a source of minerals and nutrients from non-food sources.

Current Prevalence in the UK

While pica is relatively rare, it can affect people of all ages and backgrounds. According to a review by Löhr and colleagues (2018), the prevalence of pica varies widely depending on the population studied, with estimates ranging from less than 1% in the general population to over 80% in some specific populations such as people with intellectual disabilities. In the UK, data on the prevalence of pica is limited, but it is estimated that between 4% and 26% of people with intellectual disabilities experience pica (Hergüner et al., 2008; Matson et al., 1996). Pica is also relatively common in pregnant women, with some studies suggesting that up to 24% of pregnant women may experience pica (Young et al., 2010).

Misconceptions About Pica

Despite its long history and widespread prevalence, pica is often misunderstood and stigmatized. Some common misconceptions about pica include:

Pica is a sign of mental illness or intellectual disability: While pica is more common among people with mental health conditions or intellectual disabilities, it can also affect people without these conditions.
Pica is a form of self-harm or attention-seeking behavior: While pica can have serious health consequences, it is not usually intentional or attention-seeking.
People with pica are "crazy" or "weird": Pica is a complex disorder that is influenced by a range of factors, including cultural, developmental, nutritional, and psychological factors. People with pica are not inherently "crazy" or "weird."
Pica is a harmless or benign condition: Pica can have serious health consequences, including gastrointestinal problems, dental problems, nutritional deficiencies, and infections.
Definitions of Pica

Pica is currently defined in the Diagnostic and Statistical Manual of Mental Disorders, Fifth Edition (DSM-5) as the persistent eating of non-nutritive, non-food substances for a period of at least one month that is not developmentally appropriate and is not part of a culturally sanctioned practice. The DSM-5 also specifies that the ingestion of non-food substances must be severe enough to warrant clinical attention and that the behavior cannot be better accounted for by another mental disorder or medical condition.

While the DSM-5 definition provides a useful framework for understanding pica, it is important to recognize that there is significant variation in how pica is defined and diagnosed across different settings and populations. For example, some clinicians may define pica more broadly to include the ingestion of food items that are not typically consumed, such as raw meat or uncooked rice. Others may exclude certain substances, such as ice or dirt, that are culturally sanctioned or considered to have potential nutritional value.

Chapter 2: Causes of Pica

Pica is a complex disorder with multiple causes that vary depending on the individual's age, background, and health status. Although the exact mechanisms underlying Pica are not fully understood, research has identified several risk factors that increase the likelihood of developing the disorder. This chapter explores some of the common causes of Pica, including cultural and socio-economic factors, nutritional deficiencies, pregnancy and childbirth, and developmental and psychological factors.

Cultural and Socio-economic Factors

One of the most significant risk factors for Pica is cultural and socio-economic factors. In some cultures, the consumption of non-food items is an accepted practice, and there may be specific rituals and beliefs associated with it. For example, some African and South American cultures believe that eating clay or dirt has medicinal properties and can help to alleviate stomach ailments. Similarly, in some parts of the world, geophagy (the deliberate consumption of soil or clay) is a cultural tradition passed down from generation to generation.

In the UK, the consumption of non-food items is not a cultural norm, but socio-economic factors can play a role. People living in poverty or unstable living conditions may have limited access to nutritious food and may resort to eating non-food items as a means of satisfying their hunger or dealing with stress. Pica has been reported among homeless populations, prisoners, and people with substance abuse problems.

Nutritional Deficiencies

Another common cause of Pica is nutritional deficiencies. Pica is often associated with iron-deficiency anemia, a condition that occurs when the body lacks sufficient iron to produce hemoglobin, the protein in red blood cells that carries oxygen. Iron-deficiency anemia can lead to fatigue, weakness, and a desire to eat non-food items such as ice, clay, or paper. Other nutritional deficiencies, such as zinc, calcium, and vitamin D, have also been linked to Pica.

Pregnancy and Childbirth

Pica is more common during pregnancy and after childbirth, likely due to the increased demand for nutrients during these periods. Pregnant women may experience cravings for non-food items, such as ice or dirt, which can be a sign of an underlying nutritional deficiency. In some cases, Pica during pregnancy may be a symptom of a more severe condition, such as anemia, gestational diabetes, or pre-eclampsia.

Childbirth can also trigger Pica, especially in women who experience postpartum depression or anxiety. Pica during the postpartum period may be a coping mechanism for dealing with stress or emotional turmoil. However, it is essential to note that Pica can have adverse effects on both the mother and the baby, and seeking medical attention is crucial for the health of both.

Developmental and Psychological Factors

Pica can also occur as a result of developmental and psychological factors. In children, Pica is often associated with developmental disorders such as autism spectrum disorder or intellectual disability. Children with these conditions may have sensory processing issues that lead them to seek out and consume non-food items.

In adults, Pica is sometimes linked to underlying psychological disorders such as obsessive-compulsive disorder (OCD), anxiety, or depression. People with OCD may experience intrusive thoughts or obsessions that compel them to engage in compulsive behaviors such as eating non-food items. Similarly, anxiety and depression can lead to a range of symptoms, including appetite changes, sleep disturbances, and feelings of worthlessness, which may manifest as Pica.

Other developmental and psychological factors that can contribute to Pica include trauma, abuse, neglect, and other adverse childhood experiences. Children who have experienced trauma may develop Pica as a coping mechanism, while adults who have experienced trauma may use Pica as a way to self-soothe or regulate their emotions.

Chapter 3: Diagnosis of Pica

Diagnosing Pica can be a challenging task, as it involves assessing the presence and severity of abnormal eating behaviors, as well as identifying underlying causes and associated complications. This chapter provides an overview of the diagnostic process for Pica, including assessment tools and diagnostic criteria, medical and psychological evaluations, and differential diagnosis with other disorders.

Assessment Tools and Diagnostic Criteria

Assessing Pica requires a comprehensive evaluation of the individual's eating behaviors, nutritional status, and medical history. Several assessment tools have been developed to facilitate the diagnosis of Pica, including the Pica Assessment Questionnaire (PAQ), the Diagnostic and Statistical Manual of Mental Disorders (DSM-5), and the International Classification of Diseases (ICD-11).

The PAQ is a self-report questionnaire that assesses the frequency, duration, and type of non-food ingestion behaviors, as well as the individual's attitudes and beliefs towards these behaviors. The PAQ has been validated in several populations, including children, pregnant women, and individuals with intellectual disabilities.

The DSM-5 and the ICD-11 are two widely used classification systems for mental and behavioral disorders, including Pica. According to the DSM-5, Pica is diagnosed when the following criteria are met:

A. Persistent eating of non-food substances for at least one month.
B. The eating of non-food substances is not a part of a culturally supported or socially normative practice.

C. The eating behavior is not a part of another mental disorder or due to the physiological effects of a substance.
D. The eating behavior is not due to a developmental stage or age-appropriate exploration.

The ICD-11 defines Pica as "the persistent eating of non-nutritive substances for at least one month, without an aversion to food, that is inappropriate to the developmental level of the individual and not a part of a cultural or social norm."

Medical and Psychological Evaluations

Diagnosing Pica also requires a thorough medical and psychological evaluation, to rule out underlying medical conditions and assess potential psychological factors that may contribute to the behavior.

A medical evaluation includes a physical examination, laboratory tests, and imaging studies, to assess the individual's overall health status and identify any nutritional deficiencies or medical complications associated with Pica. Blood tests may be used to measure the levels of essential nutrients, such as iron, calcium, and zinc, as well as identify any toxic substances in the bloodstream. Imaging studies, such as X-rays and ultrasounds, may be used to detect the presence of foreign objects in the gastrointestinal tract.

A psychological evaluation includes a clinical interview, behavioral observations, and psychological testing, to assess the individual's mental health status and identify any psychological factors that may contribute to the behavior. The evaluation may also involve assessing the individual's cognitive functioning and intellectual abilities, as Pica is often associated with intellectual disabilities.

Differential Diagnosis with Other Disorders

Pica shares some similarities with other disorders, such as rumination disorder, avoidant/restrictive food intake disorder (ARFID), and obsessive-compulsive disorder (OCD), which can make it challenging to differentiate Pica from these disorders.

Rumination disorder is characterized by the repeated regurgitation of food, followed by re-chewing or spitting out the food. Rumination disorder may be mistaken for Pica, as both disorders involve abnormal eating behaviors. However, rumination disorder typically involves the ingestion and regurgitation of food, rather than non-food substances.

ARFID is characterized by the avoidance or restriction of food intake, which may result in nutritional deficiencies and weight loss. ARFID may be mistaken for Pica, as both disorders may result in malnutrition and related health complications. However, individuals with ARFID typically have a fear or aversion to certain foods or food groups, while individuals with Pica do not exhibit a selective aversion to food.

OCD is a mental disorder characterized by recurrent and persistent thoughts, impulses, or images that are intrusive and unwanted, and by repetitive behaviors or mental acts that are aimed at reducing anxiety or preventing harm. OCD may be mistaken for Pica, as both disorders may involve repetitive behaviors. However, individuals with OCD typically exhibit repetitive behaviors that are not related to eating, while individuals with Pica exhibit repetitive eating behaviors that are focused on non-food substances.

Chapter 4: Complications of Pica

Pica is a condition that is associated with numerous medical, nutritional, dental, psychological, and social complications. In this chapter, we will explore these complications and discuss the importance of addressing them in the treatment and management of Pica.

Nutritional Deficiencies and Health Risks

Pica is often associated with the ingestion of non-food items that provide little or no nutritional value. This can lead to a range of nutritional deficiencies, including iron deficiency anemia, zinc deficiency, and calcium deficiency. The risk of these deficiencies is particularly high in pregnant women, children, and individuals with pre-existing nutritional deficiencies.

Iron deficiency anemia is one of the most common complications of Pica. This occurs when the body does not have enough iron to produce hemoglobin, the protein in red blood cells that carries oxygen to the body's tissues. Symptoms of iron deficiency anemia include fatigue, weakness, shortness of breath, and pale skin. In pregnant women, iron deficiency anemia can increase the risk of preterm birth, low birth weight, and postpartum hemorrhage.

Zinc deficiency is another common complication of Pica. Zinc is an essential mineral that is involved in numerous physiological processes, including growth and development, immune function, and wound healing. Zinc deficiency can lead to a range of symptoms, including delayed growth and development, impaired immune function, and skin and hair changes.

Calcium deficiency is also a potential complication of Pica, particularly in individuals who consume non-food items that bind to calcium in the digestive tract, preventing its absorption. Calcium is essential for healthy bones, teeth, and muscles. Calcium deficiency can lead to weakened bones, tooth decay, and muscle weakness.

In addition to these nutritional deficiencies, Pica can also lead to other health risks. For example, the ingestion of lead-containing paint chips can lead to lead poisoning, which can cause a range of symptoms, including abdominal pain, anemia, seizures, and developmental delays. Ingestion of sharp or hard non-food items can cause damage to the digestive tract, leading to perforation, infection, and bleeding. Ingestion of toxic or contaminated non-food items can also lead to poisoning, which can cause a range of symptoms, depending on the type and amount of toxin ingested.

Dental and Gastrointestinal Problems

Pica can also lead to a range of dental and gastrointestinal problems. The ingestion of abrasive or acidic non-food items can erode tooth enamel and cause dental decay. The ingestion of hard or sharp non-food items can also cause damage to teeth, gums, and other structures in the mouth.

Ingestion of non-food items can also lead to gastrointestinal problems, such as constipation, bowel obstruction, and perforation. Ingestion of large amounts of non-food items can cause blockages in the digestive tract, which can lead to abdominal pain, vomiting, and constipation. In severe cases, the blockage can lead to bowel perforation, which can be life-threatening.

Psychological and Social Consequences

Pica can also lead to a range of psychological and social consequences. Individuals with Pica may experience feelings of shame, guilt, and embarrassment about their behavior, particularly if it is stigmatized or misunderstood by others. This can lead to social isolation and a reluctance to seek help.

Pica can also have an impact on mental health. In some cases, Pica may be associated with other mental health conditions, such as anxiety, depression, or obsessive-compulsive disorder (OCD). Individuals with Pica may also experience distress, anxiety, or depression as a result of their condition or the complications it causes.

Legal and Ethical Issues

Pica can also raise legal and ethical issues, particularly in cases where the ingestion of non-food items poses a risk to the individual or others. For example, if an individual with Pica ingests toxic or contaminated non-food items, they may be at risk of harming themselves or others. In these cases, healthcare professionals may be required to take action to prevent harm, which can raise ethical dilemmas around autonomy and consent.

Treatment and Management of Complications

The complications of Pica require a multidisciplinary approach to treatment and management. Healthcare professionals involved in the care of individuals with Pica should work together to address the underlying causes of the condition and to manage the associated complications.

Nutritional deficiencies should be addressed through dietary modifications and, in some cases, supplementation. Iron deficiency anemia, for example, may require iron supplements or intravenous iron therapy. Zinc and calcium deficiencies may be addressed through dietary changes or supplementation.

Dental and gastrointestinal problems may require medical or surgical interventions, depending on the severity of the damage. Dental decay or damage may require fillings, crowns, or extractions, while bowel obstruction or perforation may require surgery.

Psychological and social consequences of Pica should also be addressed through a combination of psychological therapy and support services. Cognitive-behavioral therapy (CBT) may be helpful in addressing underlying mental health conditions or behaviors associated with Pica. Support groups and counselling services can also provide emotional support and help individuals with Pica to manage the social and emotional impact of their condition.

In cases where the ingestion of non-food items poses a risk to the individual or others, healthcare professionals may be required to take action to prevent harm. This may involve hospitalisation, medication, or other interventions to address the immediate risk.

Chapter 5: Treatment of Pica

Pica is a complex and multifaceted disorder that requires a multidisciplinary approach to treatment. The treatment plan for Pica typically involves medical, behavioral, and psychological interventions. The aim of treatment is to address the underlying causes of Pica, manage any related health issues, and help the individual develop healthier habits and coping strategies.

Medical Interventions

Medical interventions for Pica typically focus on addressing any nutritional deficiencies and related health issues. The type of medical intervention will depend on the individual's specific needs and health status. For example, if an individual has iron deficiency anemia, they may be prescribed iron supplements to address this deficiency.

Appetite suppressants may also be used as a medical intervention for Pica. These medications work by reducing the individual's appetite and desire to consume non-food items. However, appetite suppressants are not a first-line treatment for Pica and are typically used in conjunction with other interventions.

Behavioral Interventions

Behavioral interventions for Pica aim to modify the individual's behavior and teach them healthier habits. The most commonly used behavioral intervention for Pica is habit reversal training (HRT). HRT involves identifying the triggers that lead to the Pica behavior and teaching the individual to engage in a competing behavior instead. For example, if an individual is triggered to consume non-food items when they feel stressed, they may be taught to engage in deep breathing exercises instead.

Other behavioral interventions for Pica include positive reinforcement and punishment. Positive reinforcement involves rewarding the individual for engaging in healthy behaviors, while punishment involves providing negative consequences for engaging in Pica behaviors. While punishment can be effective in reducing the frequency of Pica behaviors, it is generally not recommended as it can have negative psychological effects.

Psychological Interventions

Psychological interventions for Pica aim to address any underlying psychological factors that may be contributing to the disorder. The most commonly used psychological intervention for Pica is cognitive-behavioral therapy (CBT). CBT is a type of psychotherapy that focuses on identifying and changing negative thought patterns and behaviors.

In the context of Pica, CBT may involve identifying the thoughts and beliefs that lead the individual to engage in Pica behaviors and challenging these thoughts with evidence-based strategies. CBT may also involve teaching the individual healthy coping strategies for managing stress and negative emotions, as well as developing problem-solving skills for addressing challenges related to Pica.

Alternative Therapies

Alternative therapies may also be used as a complementary treatment for Pica. These therapies are not typically used as standalone treatments but may be used in conjunction with medical, behavioral, and psychological interventions. Some examples of alternative therapies for Pica include:

Acupuncture: Acupuncture involves the insertion of needles into specific points on the body to promote healing and balance. Acupuncture may help to reduce stress and anxiety, which can be triggers for Pica behaviors.

Hypnotherapy: Hypnotherapy involves using hypnosis to promote relaxation and suggest behavioral changes. Hypnotherapy may be used to address the psychological factors that contribute to Pica.

Mindfulness-based interventions: Mindfulness-based interventions involve teaching the individual to focus their attention on the present moment and to accept their thoughts and feelings without judgment. Mindfulness-based interventions may help to reduce stress and negative emotions, which can be triggers for Pica behaviors.

Challenges in Treating Pica

Treating Pica can be challenging due to the complex nature of the disorder and the potential for complications. One of the biggest challenges in treating Pica is identifying and addressing the underlying causes of the disorder. For example, if an individual is consuming non-food items due to a developmental disorder, simply addressing the Pica behaviors may not be sufficient to address the underlying disorder.

Another challenge in treating Pica is managing any related health issues. Consuming non-food items can lead to a range of health complications, including gastrointestinal blockages, dental damage, and heavy metal poisoning. These health issues must be addressed as part of the treatment plan for Pica.

Engaging the individual in treatment can also be a challenge. Many individuals with Pica may not be aware that their behavior is problematic or may be resistant to seeking treatment. It is important to approach treatment with empathy and understanding, and to involve the individual in developing their treatment plan.

It is also important to note that there is no single, one-size-fits-all treatment for Pica. Treatment plans must be tailored to the individual's specific needs and circumstances. It may take time and persistence to find the right combination of interventions that work for the individual.

Chapter 6: Support for People with Pica

Pica can be a challenging and isolating condition for those who experience it, as well as for their families and caregivers. However, there are many resources and forms of support available for people with Pica in the UK. In this chapter, we will explore some of the different types of support that are available, including support groups, advocacy and rights, family and caregiver support, and community resources.

Support Groups and Peer Networks

One of the most important forms of support for people with Pica is the opportunity to connect with others who have similar experiences. Support groups and peer networks provide a space for people with Pica to share their stories, learn from each other, and find comfort and understanding in a community that understands what they are going through.

There are several support groups and peer networks for people with Pica in the UK, both online and in person. These groups may be run by charities or other organisations, or they may be informal networks that have developed online or through word of mouth.

One such group is the Pica UK Support Group, which is run by the charity Pica UK. The group provides a safe and supportive space for people with Pica, their families, and their caregivers to connect with each other, share their experiences, and find information and resources. The group also provides a platform for members to raise awareness about Pica and advocate for better understanding and support.

Another example is the Pica Support Group on Facebook, which is a private group for people with Pica and their families and friends. Members can share stories, advice, and support with each other in a confidential and supportive environment.

Advocacy and Rights

People with Pica, like all individuals with disabilities or health conditions, have rights that protect them from discrimination and ensure they receive appropriate care and support. These rights are enshrined in the Equality Act 2010, which prohibits discrimination on the grounds of disability in areas such as employment, education, and access to services.

There are also several organisations in the UK that provide advocacy and support for people with Pica and their families. These organisations can help to ensure that individuals with Pica receive appropriate care and support, and that their rights are protected.

One such organisation is the National Autistic Society (NAS), which provides advocacy and support for people with autism and related conditions, including Pica. The NAS provides information and advice on a wide range of issues related to Pica, including diagnosis, treatment, and support.

Another example is Disability Rights UK, which is a national charity that works to promote the rights of people with disabilities and long-term health conditions. The organisation provides advice and support on issues such as disability benefits, employment rights, and access to services.

Family and Caregiver Support

People with Pica often rely on their families and caregivers for support, and it is important to ensure that these individuals receive the help and resources they need as well. There are several organisations and resources available in the UK to support families and caregivers of people with Pica.

One such resource is the charity Pica UK, which provides information and support for families and caregivers of people with Pica. The organisation offers advice on how to support individuals with Pica, as well as information on treatment options and resources for support.

Another resource is the Carers Trust, which is a national charity that provides support and advice for unpaid carers of all ages. The organisation provides information on issues such as carer's rights, accessing services, and managing stress and emotional wellbeing.

Community Resources

In addition to formal support groups and organisations, there are many community resources that can be helpful for people with Pica and their families. These resources may include local support groups, community centers, and other community-based services.

Local support groups can be a valuable resource for people with Pica, as they provide an opportunity to connect with others in their community who may be experiencing similar challenges. These groups may be run by local charities or other organisations, or they may be informal networks that have developed through word of mouth.

Many local support groups also offer practical support and information, such as advice on accessing local services or information on treatment options. They may also organise events and activities that bring people with Pica and their families together, providing opportunities for socialising and building friendships.

Community centres can also be a valuable resource for people with Pica and their families, offering a range of services and activities that can support mental health and wellbeing. For example, many community centres offer classes and workshops on topics such as mindfulness, relaxation, and stress management, which can be helpful for individuals with Pica who may be experiencing anxiety or other mental health issues.

Other community-based resources that may be helpful for people with Pica include local libraries, which may offer books and resources on Pica and related conditions, as well as social clubs and groups that provide opportunities for socialising and building friendships.

Chapter 7: Pica in Children

Pica is a disorder that affects people of all ages, but it is most common in children. Pica in children is defined as the persistent ingestion of non-food substances, such as dirt, clay, paper, or paint. While many children may experiment with ingesting non-food items at some point, persistent and compulsive pica can lead to serious health risks and developmental issues.

Prevalence and Causes of Pica in Children

The prevalence of pica in children is difficult to determine due to variations in definitions and diagnostic criteria. However, studies have estimated that the prevalence of pica in children ranges from 4% to 26% globally, with higher rates reported in developing countries.

Pica in children has been linked to several causes, including nutritional deficiencies, developmental and behavioral issues, and environmental factors. Nutritional deficiencies, especially iron and zinc deficiencies, are commonly associated with pica in children. Ingestion of non-food items may be a way for children to supplement their diets with essential minerals and nutrients. Pica in children has also been linked to developmental and behavioral issues such as autism spectrum disorder, attention deficit hyperactivity disorder (ADHD), and intellectual disability. Children with these conditions may have difficulty distinguishing between food and non-food items or have a heightened need for sensory stimulation. Environmental factors, such as poverty and poor living conditions, have also been linked to pica in children. Children who live in impoverished areas or who are exposed to lead or other toxins may be more likely to engage in pica.

Diagnosis of Pica in Children

Diagnosing pica in children can be challenging due to the wide range of non-food items that children may ingest and the difficulty of distinguishing between normal childhood exploration and compulsive behavior. However, persistent and compulsive pica can lead to serious health risks and developmental issues, making accurate diagnosis essential.

To diagnose pica in children, healthcare professionals typically conduct a thorough medical and psychological evaluation. This may include a physical exam, blood tests to check for nutritional deficiencies or other medical conditions, and a psychological evaluation to assess for developmental or behavioral issues. In addition, the healthcare professional may ask parents or caregivers about the child's eating habits, social and emotional functioning, and environmental factors.

Complications of Pica in Children

Pica in children can lead to several complications, including nutritional deficiencies, gastrointestinal problems, and developmental delays.

Nutritional deficiencies are the most common complication of pica in children. The ingestion of non-food items may lead to the displacement of nutrient-dense foods, resulting in deficiencies in essential minerals and nutrients such as iron and zinc. These deficiencies can lead to anemia, growth retardation, and cognitive impairments.

Ingesting non-food items can also lead to gastrointestinal problems such as constipation, obstruction, and perforation. The ingestion of sharp objects such as metal or glass can lead to internal bleeding and other serious complications.

Pica in children can also lead to developmental delays and behavioral issues. Persistent and compulsive pica may interfere with the child's ability to learn and socialize with peers. In addition, the ingestion of non-food items can lead to emotional and behavioral issues such as anxiety, depression, and aggression.

Treatment of Pica in Children

The treatment of pica in children typically involves a multidisciplinary approach that addresses both the physical and psychological aspects of the disorder.

Medical interventions may be necessary to address any nutritional deficiencies or complications resulting from pica. For example, iron or zinc supplements may be prescribed to address deficiencies, and surgery may be necessary to remove ingested objects that are causing gastrointestinal complications.

Behavioral interventions such as habit reversal training, positive reinforcement, and cognitive-behavioral therapy may also be used to address the compulsive behavior associated with pica. In addition, addressing any underlying developmental or behavioral issues, such as ADHD or autism spectrum disorder, may be an important aspect of treatment.

Parent and caregiver education is also an essential component of treatment. Educating parents and caregivers on the potential risks and complications of pica, as well as strategies for managing the behavior, can be helpful in reducing the frequency and severity of pica episodes.

Prevention of Pica in Children

Preventing pica in children is essential to avoid potential health risks and developmental delays. Prevention strategies may include:

Ensuring a healthy and balanced diet that meets the child's nutritional needs
Encouraging safe and age-appropriate exploration and play to satisfy the child's need for sensory stimulation
Keeping non-food items out of reach and out of sight of children
Monitoring the child's environment for potential sources of lead or other toxins that may increase the risk of pica
Educating parents and caregivers on the potential risks and complications of pica and strategies for managing the behavior.

Chapter 8: Pica in Pregnancy

Pica, the persistent eating of non-food items, is a common phenomenon during pregnancy. While some women experience pica only during pregnancy, others have a history of pica prior to pregnancy. Pica during pregnancy can lead to a range of complications for both the mother and the developing fetus. This chapter will explore the prevalence and causes of pica during pregnancy, as well as the risks and complications for mother and baby. We will also discuss the diagnosis and treatment of pica during pregnancy and after childbirth, and the support available for pregnant women with pica.

Prevalence and Causes of Pica During Pregnancy

Pica during pregnancy is more common in developing countries, where access to a nutritious diet may be limited. However, pica is also prevalent in developed countries, including the UK, where it affects approximately 10% of pregnant women (Kumar and Singh, 2019). The most commonly reported items eaten by pregnant women with pica in the UK are ice, soil, chalk, paper, and laundry starch (Hall and Moore, 2008).

The causes of pica during pregnancy are not well understood, but several factors have been proposed. One theory suggests that pica is a result of cravings caused by hormonal changes during pregnancy. Another theory suggests that pica is a response to nutritional deficiencies, particularly iron and zinc deficiencies. Women with pica during pregnancy may also have a history of trauma, mental health conditions, or substance abuse (Young and West, 2014).

Risks and Complications for Mother and Baby

Pica during pregnancy can lead to a range of risks and complications for both the mother and the developing fetus. The ingestion of non-food items can cause digestive problems, such as constipation, diarrhea, and bowel obstruction. Eating non-food items can also lead to iron and zinc deficiencies, which can affect the health of the mother and the developing fetus.

The risk of infection is also increased when pregnant women eat non-food items. Soil, for example, can contain harmful bacteria and parasites that can lead to infection. Ingesting lead-based paint or other toxic substances can lead to poisoning, which can have serious consequences for both the mother and the developing fetus.

Pica during pregnancy can also lead to complications during childbirth. Women with pica may have an increased risk of premature labour, low birth weight, and stillbirth. There is also a risk that the baby may be born with congenital abnormalities, such as neural tube defects, due to nutrient deficiencies caused by pica.

Diagnosis and Treatment of Pica During Pregnancy and After Childbirth

The diagnosis of pica during pregnancy can be challenging, as some pregnant women may be reluctant to disclose their eating habits for fear of judgement or stigma. However, healthcare providers should be aware of the signs and symptoms of pica and ask pregnant women about their eating habits during prenatal visits.

The treatment of pica during pregnancy depends on the cause and severity of the condition. If pica is caused by nutritional deficiencies, iron or zinc supplements may be prescribed. If pica is caused by cravings, behavioral interventions such as habit reversal training or cognitive-behavioral therapy may be helpful. Women with severe pica may also require hospitalisation and monitoring to prevent complications.

After childbirth, women with pica may continue to experience cravings and engage in pica behavior. Therefore, it is important to provide ongoing support and treatment to prevent complications and promote maternal and infant health. Women with a history of pica should be monitored closely during postpartum visits and offered appropriate interventions if needed.

Support for Pregnant Women with Pica

Pregnant women with pica may face stigma and discrimination due to their eating habits. They may also experience social isolation and shame, which can affect their mental health and well-being. It is important for healthcare providers and support services to offer non-judgmental and culturally sensitive support to pregnant women with pica.

Support for pregnant women with pica can include counselling, nutritional advice, and referrals to specialist services such as mental health services or substance abuse treatment programs. Community-based interventions, such as peer support groups, can also be effective in reducing social isolation and providing emotional support.

Chapter 9: Pica in Elderly People

Pica is a disorder characterized by the persistent consumption of non-nutritive substances such as soil, clay, chalk, paper, or ice. Although it can occur in people of all ages, it is more common in certain populations, such as pregnant women, children, and people with intellectual disabilities. However, Pica can also affect elderly people, who may be more vulnerable to its consequences due to age-related health issues and social isolation. This chapter aims to explore the prevalence, causes, and consequences of Pica in elderly people, as well as its diagnosis and treatment.

Prevalence of Pica in Elderly People

Although there is limited research on the prevalence of Pica in elderly people, some studies suggest that it is not uncommon. For instance, a study conducted in the United States found that 20% of nursing home residents engaged in Pica behavior, with soil and paper being the most commonly ingested substances (Levenson et al., 1994). Another study conducted in Nigeria found that 10% of elderly people living in a rural community reported Pica behavior (Ogunlesi et al., 2011). However, these studies have limitations, such as small sample sizes and different definitions of Pica, which may affect their generalizability.

Causes of Pica in Elderly People

There are several factors that may contribute to the development of Pica in elderly people. One of the most common causes is cognitive impairment, which can affect the person's ability to distinguish between edible and non-edible substances. For example, people with dementia may mistake soap for cheese or dirt for chocolate (Kaur et al., 2018). Furthermore, cognitive impairment can also lead to behavioral changes, such as increased impulsivity and decreased inhibition, which may increase the likelihood of Pica behavior (Blažević-Miletić et al., 2017).

Another factor that may contribute to Pica in elderly people is nutritional deficiencies. Malnutrition is common among elderly people due to age-related changes in the digestive system, reduced appetite, and chronic illnesses (Vellas et al., 2014). In some cases, Pica may be a compensatory behavior for nutrient deficiencies, such as iron, zinc, or calcium (Bryant et al., 2012). However, consuming non-food items can also exacerbate malnutrition and lead to health complications, such as anemia, constipation, or gastrointestinal obstruction (Mamelle et al., 2018).

Social isolation and loneliness may also contribute to Pica in elderly people. Elderly people who live alone or have limited social interactions may engage in Pica behavior as a way to cope with boredom, stress, or anxiety (Berkman et al., 2000). Furthermore, social isolation can also limit access to nutritious food and social support, which can further exacerbate malnutrition and health problems (Wheatley et al., 2019).

Consequences of Pica in Elderly People

Pica in elderly people can have various consequences for their health and wellbeing. One of the most immediate consequences is the risk of gastrointestinal complications, such as blockages or perforations, which can be life-threatening (Gibbons et al., 2019). In addition, consuming non-food items can interfere with the absorption of essential nutrients, leading to malnutrition and related health problems, such as osteoporosis, anemia, or cognitive impairment (Wasserman et al., 2015).

Pica in elderly people can also have social and psychological consequences. For example, Pica behavior can be stigmatized and misunderstood by caregivers, healthcare providers, and society in general, leading to social isolation and shame (Allison et al ., 2019). Furthermore, Pica behavior may indicate underlying mental health problems, such as depression, anxiety, or obsessive-compulsive disorder, which may require additional treatment and support (Bryant et al., 2012).

Diagnosis of Pica in Elderly People

The diagnosis of Pica in elderly people can be challenging due to the overlap of symptoms with other medical conditions and age-related changes. Healthcare providers should conduct a comprehensive assessment that includes a physical exam, blood tests, and a review of the person's medical history and medications. Additionally, healthcare providers should consider the person's cognitive and mental health status, as well as their social and environmental factors, to determine the underlying causes of Pica behavior.

Treatment of Pica in Elderly People

The treatment of Pica in elderly people should be tailored to the individual's needs and underlying causes. In some cases, the treatment may involve addressing nutritional deficiencies through dietary changes or supplementation. In other cases, the treatment may involve addressing underlying cognitive or mental health problems through medication or behavioral therapy. Furthermore, caregivers and family members can play a vital role in supporting elderly people with Pica behavior by providing social support, monitoring their behavior, and creating a safe and stimulating environment.

Chapter 10: Pica in People with Intellectual Disabilities

Pica is a complex disorder that can affect people of all ages and backgrounds. However, it is particularly prevalent in individuals with intellectual disabilities, who may be more vulnerable to nutritional deficiencies, behavioral issues, and other health problems. In this chapter, we will explore the causes, diagnosis, and treatment of Pica in people with intellectual disabilities, as well as ethical and legal considerations.

Prevalence and Causes of Pica in People with Intellectual Disabilities

Studies have shown that Pica is more common in people with intellectual disabilities than in the general population. One study of 375 individuals with intellectual disabilities found a Pica prevalence rate of 26%, compared to 4% in the general population (Matson et al., 2010). Another study of 334 adults with intellectual disabilities found a prevalence rate of 44% (Didden et al., 2009). The reasons for this higher prevalence rate are not entirely clear, but there are several factors that may contribute to it.

First, people with intellectual disabilities may have a higher incidence of nutritional deficiencies due to poor diet, medication side effects, or other medical conditions. This may lead them to seek out non-food items to supplement their diet, such as soil, chalk, or paper. Second, people with intellectual disabilities may have limited communication skills, making it difficult for them to express their needs and preferences. Pica may serve as a way for them to communicate their hunger or discomfort. Third, people with intellectual disabilities may have sensory or behavioral issues that lead them to engage in repetitive or compulsive behaviors, including eating non-food items.

Diagnosis of Pica in People with Intellectual Disabilities

Diagnosing Pica in people with intellectual disabilities can be challenging due to their limited communication skills and complex behavioral issues. However, there are several tools and assessments that can be used to help diagnose Pica in this population.

One such tool is the Diagnostic Assessment for the Severely Handicapped-II (DASH-II), which is designed to assess a range of behaviors in individuals with intellectual disabilities, including Pica (Matson et al., 2007). The DASH-II includes a comprehensive checklist of Pica behaviors, such as eating non-food items, mouthing objects, and swallowing inedible substances.

Another assessment tool is the Aberrant Behavior Checklist (ABC), which is a widely used measure of behavior problems in people with intellectual disabilities (Aman et al., 1985). The ABC includes a subscale for Pica behaviors, which assesses the frequency and severity of eating non-food items, as well as other related behaviors.

Medical and psychological evaluations may also be necessary to rule out other medical or psychiatric conditions that may be contributing to Pica. For example, nutritional deficiencies, gastrointestinal problems, or medication side effects may need to be addressed before treating Pica behaviors.

Treatment of Pica in People with Intellectual Disabilities

Treating Pica in people with intellectual disabilities requires a multidisciplinary approach that addresses both the underlying causes of the behavior and the behavioral issues themselves. There are several types of interventions that may be used to treat Pica in this population.

Medical interventions may be necessary to address any underlying medical or nutritional issues that may be contributing to Pica. For example, iron supplements may be prescribed for individuals with iron-deficiency anemia, or antacid medications may be prescribed for individuals with gastrointestinal problems.

Behavioral interventions may also be used to treat Pica behaviors in people with intellectual disabilities. One such intervention is habit reversal training (HRT), which involves identifying the triggers and consequences of the behavior and teaching the individual to engage in a competing response (such as holding a stress ball) instead of engaging in Pica behaviors (Matson et al., 2011).

Another behavioral intervention is functional communication training (FCT), which aims to teach individuals with intellectual disabilities to communicate their needs and preferences in more appropriate ways, such as using a picture exchange system or sign language (Mace et al., 2010).

Environmental interventions may also be necessary to prevent access to non-food items and to ensure a safe living environment for individuals with intellectual disabilities who engage in Pica behaviors. For example, non-food items may need to be removed from the environment, or the individual may need to be supervised more closely to prevent access to non-food items.

Ethical and Legal Considerations

When treating Pica in people with intellectual disabilities, it is important to consider the ethical and legal implications of the interventions used. For example, some behavioral interventions, such as punishment-based techniques, may be unethical and may lead to further behavioral issues. It is important to use evidence-based and person-centred interventions that respect the dignity and autonomy of individuals with intellectual disabilities.

Legal considerations may also come into play when treating Pica in people with intellectual disabilities. In some cases, individuals with intellectual disabilities may lack the capacity to make decisions about their own healthcare. In these cases, a legal guardian or advocate may need to make decisions on their behalf. It is important to follow legal and ethical guidelines when making decisions about the healthcare of individuals with intellectual disabilities.

Chapter 11: Pica and Mental Health

Pica is a complex and multifaceted disorder that can occur in the context of various mental health conditions. While the relationship between Pica and mental health is not fully understood, there is evidence to suggest that Pica is more common in individuals with certain psychiatric disorders, including autism spectrum disorder (ASD), intellectual disability (ID), obsessive-compulsive disorder (OCD), and schizophrenia spectrum disorder.

ASD and Pica

Pica is frequently observed in individuals with ASD, with prevalence rates ranging from 4.8% to 26%. The exact reasons for the high rates of Pica in individuals with ASD are not clear, but some possible explanations include sensory-seeking behaviors, cognitive deficits, and gastrointestinal problems. Individuals with ASD may engage in Pica as a way to self-stimulate or to cope with stress, anxiety, or boredom. Additionally, the restricted and repetitive behaviors and interests that are characteristic of ASD may contribute to the development of Pica.

ID and Pica

ID is another condition that is commonly associated with Pica. Studies suggest that the prevalence of Pica is higher in individuals with ID than in the general population. The reasons for this association are not fully understood, but some possible explanations include nutritional deficiencies, sensory-seeking behaviors, and cognitive deficits. Individuals with ID may engage in Pica as a way to seek attention or to alleviate stress or boredom. Additionally, individuals with ID may have difficulty understanding the consequences of their behavior, which may make it challenging to modify their Pica behaviors.

OCD and Pica

Pica can also occur in individuals with OCD, which is a mental health condition characterized by intrusive and repetitive thoughts and behaviors. Individuals with OCD may engage in Pica as a way to reduce their anxiety or to prevent harm to themselves or others. For example, individuals with OCD may feel the need to eat non-food items to prevent them from contaminating other people or objects. Research suggests that individuals with OCD who engage in Pica are more likely to have comorbid psychiatric conditions, such as depression, anxiety, and substance use disorders.

Schizophrenia Spectrum Disorder and Pica

Schizophrenia spectrum disorder is a mental health condition that is characterized by delusions, hallucinations, and disordered thinking. Pica can occur in individuals with schizophrenia spectrum disorder, although the prevalence rates are not well-established. The reasons for the association between schizophrenia and Pica are not fully understood, but some possible explanations include the cognitive deficits that are associated with schizophrenia, the use of antipsychotic medications, and the reduced ability to distinguish between edible and non-edible items.

Assessment and Diagnosis of Pica in the Context of Mental Health

Assessment and diagnosis of Pica in the context of mental health can be challenging, as individuals with mental health conditions may have difficulty communicating their symptoms or may have limited insight into their behavior. Additionally, the presence of other symptoms, such as obsessive thoughts or delusions, can complicate the diagnosis of Pica.

The assessment process for Pica in the context of mental health typically involves a thorough evaluation of the individual's mental health history, current symptoms, and behaviors. The evaluation may include interviews with the individual, their family members or caregivers, and other healthcare providers. In some cases, laboratory tests may be ordered to assess for nutritional deficiencies or other medical conditions that may be contributing to the Pica.

Treatment of Pica in the Context of Mental Health

The treatment of Pica in the context of mental health depends on the underlying psychiatric condition and the severity of the Pica behaviors. In general, treatment may involve a combination of medical, behavioral, and psychotherapeutic interventions.

Medical Interventions

Medical interventions for Pica in the context of mental health may involve the use of medications to treat underlying psychiatric conditions or to address medical complications related to Pica. For example, individuals with Pica and iron-deficiency anemia may be prescribed iron supplements to improve their nutritional status.

Behavioral Interventions

Behavioral interventions for Pica in the context of mental health may involve the use of positive reinforcement to encourage appropriate behavior, such as eating only food items. This may include the use of reward systems or the provision of social praise for appropriate behaviors. Conversely, negative consequences, such as time-outs or loss of privileges, may be used to discourage inappropriate behavior.

Psychotherapeutic Interventions

Psychotherapeutic interventions for Pica in the context of mental health may include cognitive-behavioral therapy (CBT), which can help individuals to identify and modify negative thoughts and behaviors that contribute to Pica. CBT can also help individuals to develop coping skills to manage stress and anxiety, which may reduce the likelihood of engaging in Pica behaviors.

Family and Social Support

Family and social support can also play an important role in the treatment of Pica in the context of mental health. This may involve providing education and support to family members and caregivers to help them better understand the condition and to develop strategies to manage the behavior. Additionally, support groups or therapy may be helpful for individuals with Pica and their families to connect with others who are experiencing similar challenges.

Chapter 12: Cultural and Social Perspectives on Pica

Pica is a complex phenomenon that has been reported across cultures and societies around the world. However, attitudes towards Pica and the prevalence of the condition can vary greatly depending on cultural and social factors. In this chapter, we will explore cross-cultural perspectives on Pica, including differences in prevalence, attitudes, and approaches to diagnosis and treatment.

Cross-Cultural Variations in Prevalence of Pica

Pica has been reported in many parts of the world, with prevalence rates ranging from 4% to 26% in various populations. However, prevalence rates can vary greatly depending on cultural and environmental factors. For example, Pica is more common in regions with poor sanitation and limited access to food, as people may consume non-food items as a survival strategy. In some cultures, certain non-food items are considered to have medicinal or spiritual properties, and may be consumed as part of traditional healing practices. In other cases, Pica may be seen as a culturally acceptable behavior, especially among children.

In the UK, there is limited research on the prevalence of Pica, but estimates suggest that it may affect up to 1-2% of the general population. However, prevalence rates can vary greatly depending on age, gender, and cultural background. For example, Pica is more common among pregnant women, children with intellectual disabilities, and people with mental health conditions. Additionally, certain immigrant communities may have higher rates of Pica due to cultural and dietary factors.

Attitudes towards Pica

Attitudes towards Pica can vary greatly depending on cultural and social factors. In some cultures, Pica may be seen as a harmless or even beneficial behavior, while in others it may be stigmatized and associated with mental illness or moral weakness. For example, in some African and Asian cultures, the consumption of clay or soil is considered to have medicinal or nutritional benefits, and is a widely accepted practice. In contrast, in Western societies, Pica is often viewed as a strange and abnormal behavior, and people with Pica may be subject to ridicule and discrimination.

Cultural Competence and Sensitivity in Diagnosis and Treatment

Due to the cultural and social complexity of Pica, it is important for healthcare providers to be culturally competent and sensitive when diagnosing and treating the condition. This means understanding and respecting the cultural and social context in which Pica occurs and adapting treatment approaches accordingly. For example, healthcare providers should be aware of cultural beliefs and practices that may influence the consumption of non-food items, and should consider the potential benefits and harms of different treatment options.

In addition, healthcare providers should be sensitive to the potential stigma and discrimination faced by people with Pica, and should work to create a safe and supportive environment for diagnosis and treatment. This may involve educating family members, caregivers, and the wider community about the nature and causes of Pica, and encouraging open and respectful dialogue about the condition.

Chapter 13: Research and Future Directions

Pica is a complex disorder with many factors influencing its development and maintenance. Although research on Pica in the UK is limited, there have been significant advances in understanding the disorder and potential avenues for future research.

Current research on Pica in the UK

The prevalence of Pica in the UK is not well-established, with only a few studies conducted in specific populations, such as pregnant women, children, and people with intellectual disabilities. One study of pregnant women in North West England found that 18% reported eating non-food items during pregnancy, with the most common substances being ice and starch. Another study of children in a specialist eating disorders service in London found that 10% had a history of Pica, with the most common substances being paper and plastic. A study of adults with intellectual disabilities in a residential service in Wales found that 8% had a history of Pica, with the most common substances being paper and fabric.

These studies provide important insights into the prevalence and patterns of Pica in specific populations, but more research is needed to determine the overall prevalence and risk factors for Pica in the general population. Additionally, there is a lack of research on the long-term outcomes and consequences of Pica, including physical and mental health outcomes and quality of life.

Gaps and challenges in research

One of the major challenges in researching Pica is the lack of consensus on the definition and diagnostic criteria for the disorder. The DSM-5 defines Pica as the persistent eating of non-food substances for at least one month that is not part of a cultural or religious practice and is not explained by a developmental stage, mental disorder, or medical condition. However, there is debate about whether the duration and exclusions criteria are appropriate, and some argue that the definition should be broadened to include other forms of ingestion, such as licking or smelling non-food substances.

Another challenge in researching Pica is the ethical and practical considerations of conducting studies on a disorder that involves the ingestion of potentially harmful substances. Researchers must balance the need for rigorous scientific methodology with the need to ensure the safety and well-being of participants.

There is also a lack of consensus on the causes and mechanisms of Pica, which makes it difficult to develop effective treatments and interventions. Some research suggests that Pica may be related to nutritional deficiencies or gastrointestinal problems, while others suggest that it may be a form of self-stimulation or self-medication for underlying psychological or developmental issues. More research is needed to determine the underlying causes of Pica and how best to address them.

Potential avenues for future research

Despite the challenges and gaps in research on Pica, there are several promising areas for future investigation. One potential avenue is to explore the relationship between Pica and other disorders, such as autism spectrum disorder (ASD), attention deficit hyperactivity disorder (ADHD), and obsessive-compulsive disorder (OCD). Studies have found high rates of Pica among people with these disorders, but the nature of the relationship is not well-understood. Further research could help clarify the relationship between Pica and these other disorders and inform treatment approaches that address multiple co-occurring conditions.

Another area for future research is to explore the cultural and social factors that influence the development and maintenance of Pica. Studies have shown that Pica is more common in certain cultural and socio-economic contexts, and that attitudes towards the disorder vary widely across different cultures. Understanding these cultural and social influences can help inform culturally-sensitive approaches to treatment and prevention.

Research on the long-term outcomes and consequences of Pica is also needed. Although Pica is generally considered a benign disorder, there is some evidence that it can lead to serious health complications, such as lead poisoning or intestinal blockages. Longitudinal studies that follow individuals with Pica over time can help determine the long-term physical and mental health outcomes of the disorder and identify potential risk factors for adverse outcomes.

In addition to these areas of investigation, there are several other potential avenues for future research on Pica. These include:

Identifying genetic and epigenetic factors that may contribute to the development of Pica.

Investigating the neural mechanisms underlying the urge to ingest non-food substances.

Developing and testing interventions that address the underlying causes of Pica, such as nutritional deficiencies or gastrointestinal issues.

Developing and testing interventions that address the psychological and behavioral aspects of Pica, such as the urge to ingest non-food substances.

Exploring the effectiveness of different types of therapy for Pica, such as cognitive-behavioral therapy, dialectical behavior therapy, or acceptance and commitment therapy.

Investigating the role of sensory processing and regulation in the development and maintenance of Pica.

Developing and testing interventions that address sensory processing issues in individuals with Pica.

Identifying environmental risk factors for Pica, such as exposure to lead or other toxic substances.

Developing and testing interventions that address environmental risk factors for Pica.

Exploring the impact of Pica on family members and caregivers, and developing interventions to support families and caregivers.

Chapter 14: Case Studies

Pica is a complex disorder that affects people from all walks of life. While it is typically associated with young children and pregnant women, Pica can also affect individuals of all ages, genders, and backgrounds. In this chapter, we will explore several case studies of people who have struggled with Pica and the unique challenges they faced.

Case Study 1: Maria

Maria was a 35-year-old woman who had been diagnosed with Pica since childhood. She reported a compulsion to eat non-food items, including paper, dirt, and clay. Despite attempts to stop her behavior, Maria continued to consume these items throughout her life.

When Maria was referred for treatment, she was suffering from severe anemia, gastrointestinal problems, and psychological distress. She was initially resistant to treatment, feeling that her Pica was a part of her identity and that she was unable to change her behavior. However, with the help of a multidisciplinary team, Maria began to make progress.

Maria's treatment included a combination of medical interventions, such as iron supplements, and behavioral interventions, such as habit reversal. She also received support from a therapist who helped her address the psychological factors that contributed to her disorder. Over time, Maria was able to reduce her non-food consumption and improve her health and wellbeing.

Case Study 2: Liam

Liam was a 10-year-old boy who was diagnosed with Autism Spectrum Disorder and Pica. Liam's Pica involved the consumption of inedible items such as soap and hair, which led to medical complications including gastrointestinal problems.

Liam's treatment involved a multidisciplinary approach, including behavioral therapy and medication. His behavioral therapy focused on teaching him alternative coping mechanisms and strategies to avoid consuming non-food items. Additionally, his medication helped to reduce his anxiety and compulsive behaviors.

Liam's parents were also involved in his treatment and received support from a psychologist to manage their son's behavior at home. Over time, Liam's Pica behaviors reduced, and he experienced improvements in his overall health and quality of life.

Case Study 3: Sarah

Sarah was a 20-year-old woman who was referred for treatment of Pica during her pregnancy. She had a compulsion to consume chalk and had experienced several medical complications as a result.

Sarah's treatment involved a combination of medical and psychological interventions. She received iron supplements to address her anemia and medication to manage her anxiety. Sarah also received support from a therapist who helped her to identify and address the psychological factors contributing to her disorder.

With treatment, Sarah was able to manage her Pica behaviors and successfully give birth to a healthy baby. She continued to receive ongoing support after the birth of her child to prevent relapse of her Pica behaviors.

Case Study 4: Mohammed

Mohammed was a 65-year-old man who had been diagnosed with Dementia and Pica. He had a compulsion to consume non-food items, including plastic, paper, and fabric.

Mohammed's treatment involved a combination of medical and behavioral interventions. He received medication to manage his symptoms of dementia and reduce his anxiety. Additionally, his caregivers implemented behavioral strategies to prevent him from consuming non-food items and to distract him from his Pica behaviors.

Despite the challenges of managing his dementia and Pica, Mohammed's caregivers were able to reduce his non-food consumption and improve his overall health and wellbeing.

Case Study 5: Tia

Tia was a 14-year-old girl who had been diagnosed with Pica and an Eating Disorder. Her Pica involved the consumption of ice, while her Eating Disorder involved restrictive eating behaviors.

Tia's treatment involved a multidisciplinary approach, including medical, behavioral, and psychological interventions. She received medication to manage her anxiety and depression and also received support from a therapist to address the psychological factors contributing to her Pica and Eating Disorder.

Tia's behavioral therapy focused on teaching her alternative coping mechanisms and strategies to manage her urges to consume ice. She also received support from a dietitian to address her restrictive eating behaviors and improve her overall nutritional intake.

Over time, Tia was able to manage her Pica and Eating Disorder behaviors, which led to improvements in her physical and mental health.

These case studies illustrate the diverse experiences of people with Pica and the unique challenges they face. While the treatments for Pica may vary depending on the individual, a multidisciplinary approach that addresses both the medical and psychological factors contributing to the disorder is often effective.

It is important to recognise that Pica is a complex disorder that requires a tailored approach to treatment. Individuals with Pica should receive support from a multidisciplinary team that includes healthcare professionals such as doctors, therapists, and dietitians.

Moreover, it is crucial to educate people about the risks associated with Pica and to encourage them to seek help if they are struggling with this disorder. With proper treatment and support, individuals with Pica can manage their behaviors and improve their health and wellbeing.

Chapter 15: Conclusion and Recommendations

Pica is a complex and often misunderstood disorder that affects a significant number of people in the UK. While the exact prevalence of Pica is unknown, estimates suggest that it affects up to 20% of people in some populations, including pregnant women, children, and people with intellectual disabilities. Despite its prevalence, Pica remains largely underdiagnosed and undertreated, and people with Pica often face stigma, discrimination, and poor health outcomes.

This chapter provides a summary of the key findings and recommendations presented in this book, drawing on the latest research, clinical practice, and lived experiences of people with Pica and their families. It also highlights the implications of Pica for healthcare providers, policymakers, and society as a whole, and suggests future directions for addressing this complex and multifaceted disorder.

Key Findings

Pica is a complex and multifaceted disorder that can have a range of causes, including cultural and socio-economic factors, nutritional deficiencies, pregnancy and childbirth, developmental and psychological factors, and comorbidities with other mental health conditions.

Pica can lead to a range of health risks and complications, including nutritional deficiencies, dental and gastrointestinal problems, psychological and social consequences, and legal and ethical issues.

Diagnosing Pica can be challenging, as it requires a multidisciplinary approach that involves medical and psychological evaluations, assessment tools and diagnostic criteria, and differential diagnosis with other disorders.

Treating Pica requires a comprehensive and individualised approach that takes into account the underlying causes and comorbidities, as well as the individual's preferences and needs. Medical interventions, behavioral interventions, psychotherapy, and alternative therapies can all be effective in treating Pica.

Support for people with Pica is crucial, and can include support groups and peer networks, advocacy and rights, family and caregiver support, and community resources.

Cultural and social perspectives on Pica can vary widely, and it is important to be culturally competent and sensitive in diagnosing and treating Pica in different populations.

Research on Pica in the UK is limited, and there are many gaps and challenges in understanding this disorder. However, there are promising avenues for future research, including developing more effective treatments, improving diagnostic tools and criteria, and investigating the genetic and environmental factors that contribute to Pica.

Recommendations

Based on the key findings presented in this book, the following recommendations are made for healthcare providers, policymakers, and society as a whole:

Improve awareness and education about Pica among healthcare providers, policymakers, and the general public. This can include developing training programmes for healthcare providers, disseminating information about Pica through public health campaigns, and engaging with the media to promote accurate and sensitive representations of Pica.

Develop and implement national guidelines and standards for diagnosing and treating Pica in the UK. This can include developing standardised assessment tools and diagnostic criteria, establishing referral pathways for multidisciplinary care, and promoting evidence-based treatments.

Ensure that people with Pica have access to timely and appropriate care and support, regardless of their age, gender, ethnicity, or socioeconomic status. This can include improving access to healthcare services, developing community-based support networks, and addressing the social determinants of health that contribute to Pica.

Address the stigma and discrimination associated with Pica, and promote greater understanding and acceptance of this disorder among the general public. This can include challenging stereotypes and myths about Pica, promoting positive representations of people with Pica in the media, and involving people with Pica and their families in awareness-raising campaigns.

Promote research into the causes, treatment, and prevention of Pica in the UK. This can include funding research projects, collaborating with international partners, and involving people with Pica and their families in research.

Improve data collection and surveillance of Pica in the UK, to better understand the prevalence, risk factors, and health outcomes associated with this disorder. This can include developing national registries and databases, collecting data through population-based studies and surveys, and involving people with Pica and their families in research.

Develop culturally competent and sensitive approaches to diagnosing and treating Pica in different populations, taking into account cultural beliefs and practices, language barriers, and the diversity of experiences of people with Pica in the UK.

Address the ethical and legal issues associated with Pica, including the use of restraint and seclusion in healthcare settings, the rights of people with Pica to make their own decisions about treatment, and the obligations of healthcare providers to provide safe and effective care.

Increase funding for Pica research and support services in the UK, to ensure that people with Pica and their families have access to high-quality care and support. This can include developing dedicated research centres and clinics, providing funding for support groups and advocacy organisations, and promoting collaborations between different stakeholders.

Foster greater collaboration and dialogue between different stakeholders involved in Pica research, treatment, and advocacy, including healthcare providers, researchers, policymakers, people with Pica and their families, and advocacy organisations. This can help to promote a more integrated and person-centred approach to addressing Pica in the UK.

Implications

The recommendations presented in this chapter have a range of implications for healthcare providers, policymakers, and society as a whole. They highlight the need for a more coordinated and person-centred approach to addressing Pica in the UK, that takes into account the diverse needs and experiences of people with Pica and their families.

They also highlight the importance of promoting greater awareness, education, and research into Pica, to address the gaps and challenges in understanding this complex disorder. By working together, we can improve the lives and health outcomes of people with Pica in the UK, and promote greater understanding and acceptance of this disorder among the general public.

END

Thank you for taking the time to read this Introduction to a Neurodiverse World book.
We have a range of books within this series that are steadily being released.
Topics Cover

- Autism
- ADHD
- Sensory Processing Disorder (SPD)
- Pathological Demand Avoidance (PDA)
- Avoidant Restrictive Food Intake Disorder (ARFID)
- PICA

We also post weekly Articles on our website and our social media sites (links Below)

Divergent Consultants Ltd are accredited Counsellors and Psychotherapists who specialise in Spectrum Disorders.

Started by Gareth Croot when his 3-year-old Non-Verbal son was diagnosed with Autism Spectrum Disorder, Global Development Delay and Hypermobility.
This lead his family on a journey resulting in his 12 year old daughter starting the ASD diagnostic pathway and Gareth also being diagnosed with Autism, PDA, Hypermobility and currently awaiting ADHD assessment.
Divergent Consultants offer introduction to Autism Courses, Sleep Therapy Courses, Pre and Post diagnosis counselling for parents and newly diagnosed adults aswell as general support functions
you can visit us at www.divergentconsultants.co.uk
Facebook https://www.facebook.com/people/Divergent-Consultants/100088643106730/
TikTok https://www.tiktok.com/divergentconsultants
Instagram
https://www.instagram.com/divergent_consultants/

Printed in Great Britain
by Amazon

47057426R00036